7.95

HORNED ANIMALS

by Cari Meister

po go

Ideas for Parents and Teachers

Pogo Books let children practice reading informational text while introducing them to nonfiction features such as headings, labels, sidebars, maps, and diagrams, as well as a table of contents, glossary, and index.

Carefully leveled text with a strong photo match offers early fluent readers the support they need to succeed.

Before Reading

- "Walk" through the book and point out the various nonfiction features. Ask the student what purpose each feature serves.
- Look at the glossary together. Read and discuss the words.

Read the Book

- Have the child read the book independently.
- Invite him or her to list questions that arise from reading.

After Reading

- Discuss the child's questions. Talk about how he or she might find answers to those questions.
- Prompt the child to think more. Ask: Have you seen any of the horned animals mentioned in the book? Can you think of any horned animals that aren't discussed?

Pogo Books are published by Jump!
5357 Penn Avenue South
Minneapolis, MN 55419
www.jumplibrary.com

Library of Congress Cataloging-in-Publication Data
Meister, Cari, author.
 Horned animals / by Cari Meister.
    pages cm. – (Back off! Animal defenses)
 Audience: Ages 7-10.
 Summary: "Carefully leveled text and vibrant photographs introduce readers to horned animals such as the kudu, yak, and cape buffalo, and explore how they use their horns to defend themselves against predators. Includes activity, glossary, and index." –Provided by publisher.
 Includes bibliographical references and index.
 ISBN 978-1-62031-310-7 (hardcover: alk. paper)
 ISBN 978-1-62496-376-6 (ebook)
 1. Horns–Juvenile literature.
 2. Animal defenses–Juvenile literature.
 3. Animal weapons–Juvenile literature.
 4. Ungulates–Juvenile literature. I. Title.
 QL759.M456 2016
 591.47–dc23

                                    2015034816

Series Editor: Jenny Fretland VanVoorst
Series Designer: Anna Peterson
Book Designer: Lindaanne Donohoe
Photo Researchers: Jenny Fretland VanVoorst and Lindaanne Donohoe

Photo Credits: Alamy, 14-15; Corbis, 5; iStock, 16; Nature Picture Library, 6-7, 17; Shutterstock, cover, 1, 3, 4, 23; SuperStock, 8-9, 10, 11, 12-13, 20-21; Thinkstock, 18-19.

Printed in the United States of America at Corporate Graphics in North Mankato, Minnesota.

TABLE OF CONTENTS

CHAPTER 1

HARD HEADED

Spotted hyenas watch as a kudu **herd grazes**. They wait for a good time to attack.

Soon the herd moves near the water. One kudu stays. He is alone. The hyenas attack. The kudu turns his head. His long, twisted horns jab. This time, the hyenas run away.

A wildebeest herd **migrates**. They stop to rest and eat. A cheetah watches. She looks for a calf, but the herd guards the young.

DID YOU KNOW?

Antlers are made of bone. They **shed** every year. Horns are made of bone and **keratin**. Horns stay on for a lifetime.

Wait! What's this? A limping wildebeest! The cheetah runs. She lunges. The wildebeest turns and **butts**. His horns are sharp. He stabs. He misses. The cheetah grabs his neck. The wildebeest goes down. This time, the cheetah wins.

CHAPTER 2
MOUNTAIN HORNS

It's **mating** season. Male big horn sheep fight. They butt their horns.

A ram's horns are massive. They weigh about 30 pounds (13.6 kilograms). That's more than all his other bones put together!

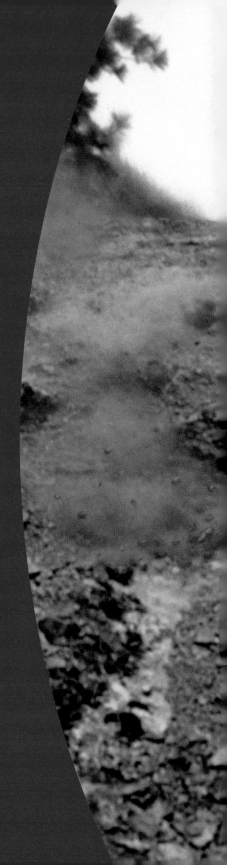

Fighting for mating rights is not the only reason sheep have horns. They use them to defend themselves against **predators**.

Here comes a puma. She **stalks**. She charges. The ram turns his head and faces the puma. He butts. The puma moves back. Then she leaps. The ram turns and runs. His horns won't help him this time.

A mountain goat climbs. Oh no! A golden eagle! She tries to grab his leg. She wants to pull him off the mountain, where he will fall to his death. But the goat has good footing. He is quick. He lowers his horns. He butts. The eagle does not want to fight. She flies away.

DID YOU KNOW?

In many kinds of goats, both males and females have horns. Male horns are always bigger.

CHAPTER 3
YAK ATTACK!

A pack of hungry wolves stalk a yak herd. A yak sees them. She grunts. She warns the leader.

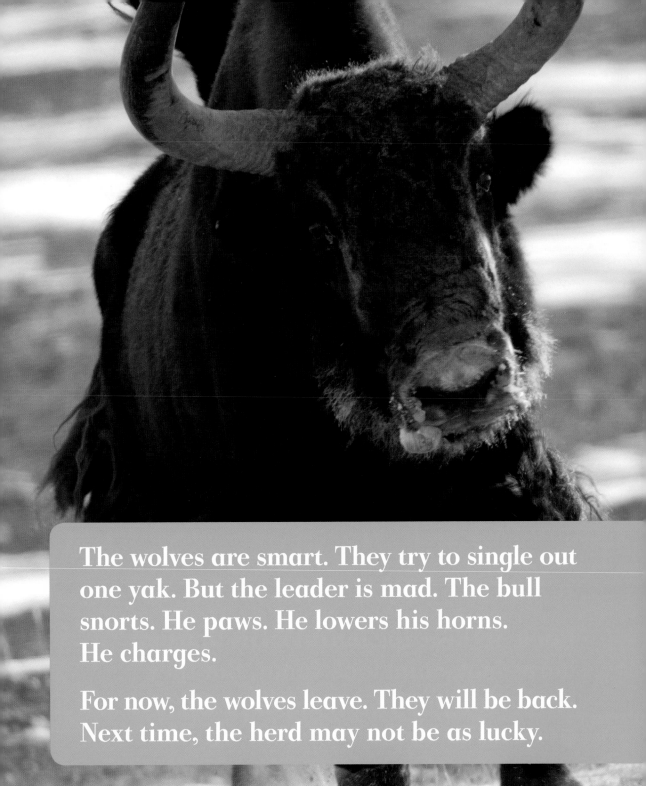

The wolves are smart. They try to single out one yak. But the leader is mad. The bull snorts. He paws. He lowers his horns. He charges.

For now, the wolves leave. They will be back. Next time, the herd may not be as lucky.

Look at this cape buffalo. His unusual horns make him look funny. But they are no laughing matter. They can **gore** an animal to death in seconds.

TAKE A LOOK!

Longest Horns:
Asian Water Buffalo
(up to 13 feet / 4 meters)

Heaviest Horns:
Watusi Bull
(up to 100 pounds /
45 kilograms)

Curliest Horns:
Spiral-horned Antelope

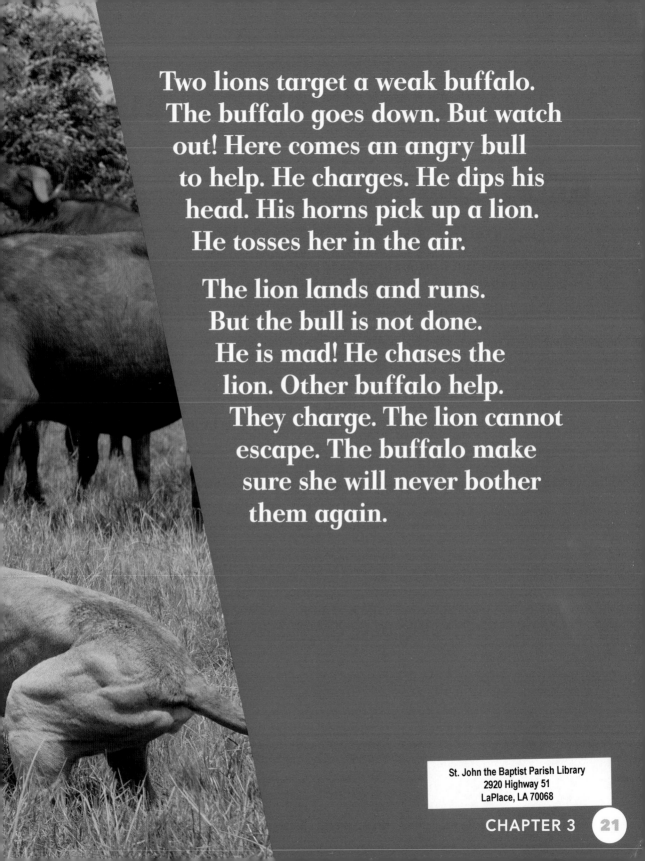

Two lions target a weak buffalo. The buffalo goes down. But watch out! Here comes an angry bull to help. He charges. He dips his head. His horns pick up a lion. He tosses her in the air.

The lion lands and runs. But the bull is not done. He is mad! He chases the lion. Other buffalo help. They charge. The lion cannot escape. The buffalo make sure she will never bother them again.

ACTIVITIES & TOOLS

WHAT'S IT LIKE TO HAVE HORNS?

Make this fun horn helmet to see what it is like to wear heavy horns. You will need:

- a bike helmet
- two empty paper towel tubes
- rocks
- duct tape

❶ Gather the materials.

❷ Duct tape the paper towel tubes onto the helmet.

❸ Fill the tubes with rocks.

❹ Duct tape the tops of the tubes so the rocks don't fall out.

❺ Put on your horned helmet!

GLOSSARY

butt: When an animal charges with their horns.

gore: To kill by making a lot of holes.

graze: To feed on grass.

herd: A group of animals that live and travel together.

keratin: A tough material; fingernails are made from keratin.

mating: The act of making babies.

migrate: To pass from one region or climate to another, usually on a regular schedule, for feeding or breeding.

predators: Animals that hunt other animals for food.

shed: To come off.

stalks: When an animal is sneaking up on another animal before it attacks.

INDEX

TO LEARN MORE

Learning more is as easy as 1, 2, 3.

1) Go to www.factsurfer.com

2) Enter "hornedanimals" into the search box.

3) Click the "Surf" button to see a list of websites.

With factsurfer, finding more information is just a click away.